FOUR INCARNATIONS

BOOKS BY ROBERT SWARD

POETRY

Advertisements, Odyssey Chapbook Number One, 1958

Uncle Dog & Other Poems, 1962

Kissing the Dancer & Other Poems, 1964

Thousand-Year-Old Fiancée & Other Poems, 1965

Horgbortom Stringbottom, I Am Yours, You Are History, 1970

Hannah's Cartoon, 1970

Quorum / Noah, 1970 (With Mike Doyle)

Gift, 1971

Five Iowa Poems, 1975

Cheers for Muktananda, 1976

Honey Bear on Lasqueti Island, B.C., 1978

Six Poems, 1980

Twelve Poems, 1982

Movies: Left to Right, 1983

Half-a-Life's History: Poems New & Selected, 1983

The Three Roberts, Premiere Performance, 1984
(Featuring Robert Priest, Robert Zend, and Robert Sward)

The Three Roberts On Love, 1985

The Three Roberts On Childhood, 1985

Poet Santa Cruz, 1985

FICTION

The Jurassic Shales, a novel, 1975

NON-FICTION

The Toronto Islands, an illustrated history, 1983

EDITED BY ROBERT SWARD

Vancouver Island Poems, an anthology, 1973

Emily Carr: The Untold Story, 1978

The publisher thanks the following organizations whose support helped make this book possible: The Bush Foundation; Minnesota State Arts Board; National Endowment for the Arts, a federal agency; Northwest Area Foundation; and Star Tribune/Cowles Media Company.

The author wishes to thank the Djerassi Foundation, the Edward MacDowell Association, Yaddo, the Cultural Council of Santa Cruz County, the John Simon Guggenheim Memorial Foundation, and the Canada Council for affording him an opportunity to complete this book.

Many of the poems in this edition appeared previously in literary magazines and reviews. A complete listing appears at the end of the book.

Coffee House Press books are available to bookstores through Consortium Book Sales and Distribution, Inc., 287 East Sixth Street, Suite 365, Saint Paul, Minnesota 55101. Our books are also available through all major library distributors and jobbers, and through most small press distributors, including Bookpeople, Bookslinger, Inland, and Small Press Distribution. For personal orders, catalogs, or information, write to:
COFFEE HOUSE PRESS
27 North Fourth Street, Suite 400, Minneapolis, Minnesota 55401

SECOND PRINTING

Library of Congress Cataloging-in-Publication Data

Sward, Robert, 1933-
    Four incarnations : new & selected poems, 1957-1991 / Robert Sward.
       p. cm.
    ISBN 0-918273-90-0 (acid-free paper) : $9.95
    I. Title.
PS3569.W3F68   1991
811'.54—dc20
                                                          91-22836
                                                             CIP

ROBERT SWARD

FOUR
INCARNATIONS

NEW & SELECTED

POEMS 1957-1991

COFFEE HOUSE PRESS

MINNEAPOLIS :: 1991

Contents

To Gloria and my children:
Cheryl, Barbara, Michael, Hannah and Nicholas

with special thanks to William Minor

Foreword:
Four Incarnations

Born on the Jewish North Side of Chicago, bar mitzvahed, sailor, amnesiac, university professor (Cornell, Iowa, Connecticut College), newspaper editor, food reviewer, father of five children, husband to four wives, my writing career has been described by critic Virginia Lee as a "long and winding road."

I. SWITCHBLADE POETRY: CHICAGO STYLE

I began writing poetry in Chicago at age 15, when I was named corresponding secretary for a gang of young punks and hoodlums called the Semcoes. A Social Athletic Club, we met at various locations two Thursdays a month. My job was to write postcards to inform my brother thugs—who carried switchblade knives and stole cars for fun and profit—as to when, where and why we were meeting.

Rhyming couplets seemed the appropriate form to notify characters like light-fingered Foxman, cross-eyed Harris, and Irving "Koko," of upcoming meetings. An example of my switchblade juvenilia:

> The Semcoes meet next Thursday night
>   at Speedway
> Koko's. Five bucks dues, Foxman, or fight.

Koko was a young boxer whose father owned Chicago's Speedway Wrecking Company and whose basement was filled with punching bags and pinball machines. Koko and the others joked about my affliction—the writing of poetry—but were so astonished that they criticized me mainly for my inability to spell.

2. SAILOR LIBRARIAN: SAN DIEGO

At 17, I graduated from high school, gave up my job as soda jerk and joined the Navy. The Korean War was underway; my mother had died, and Chicago seemed an oppressive place to be.

My thanks to the U.S. Navy. They taught me how to type (60 words a minute), organize an office, and serve as a librarian. In 1952 I served in Korea aboard a 300-foot-long, flat-bottomed Landing Ship Tank (LST). A Yeoman 3rd Class, I became overseer of 1,200 paperback books, a sturdy upright typewriter, and a couple of filing cabinets.

The best thing about duty on an LST is the ship's speed: 8 to 10 knots. It takes approximately one month for an LST to sail between San Diego and Pusan, Korea. In that month I read *Moby Dick, Leaves of Grass, Walden, Winter's Tales,* the King James version of the Bible, *Hamlet, King Lear,* and a biography of Abraham Lincoln.

While at sea, I began writing poetry as if poems, to paraphrase Thoreau, were secret letters from some distant land. I sent one poem to a girl named Lorelei with whom I was in love. Lorelei had a job at the Dairy Queen. Shortly before enlisting in the Navy, I spent $15 of my soda jerk money taking her up in a single-engine, sight-seeing airplane so we could kiss and—at the same time—get a good look at Chicago from the air. Beautiful Lorelei never responded to my poem. Years later, at the University of Iowa Writers' Workshop, I learned that much of what I had been writing (love poems inspired by a combination of lust and loneliness) belonged, loosely speaking, to a tradition—the venerable tradition of unrequited love.

3. MR. AMNESIA: CAMBRIDGE

In 1962, after ten years of writing poetry, my book, *Uncle Dog & Other Poems,* was published by Putnam in England. That was followed by two books from Cornell University Press, *Kissing the Dancer* and *Thousand-Year-Old Fiancée.* Then in 1966, I was invited to do 14 poetry readings in a two-week stretch at places like Dartmouth, Amherst, and the University of Connecticut.

The day before I was scheduled to embark on the reading series, I was hit by a speeding MG in Cambridge, Massachusetts.

I lost my memory for a period of about 24 hours. Just as I saw the world fresh while cruising to a war zone, so I now caught a glimpse of what a city like Cambridge can look like when one's inner slate, so to speak, is wiped clean.

4. SANTA CLAUS: SANTA CRUZ

In December 1985, recently returned to the U.S. after some years in Canada, a free-lance writer in search of a story, I sought and found employment as a Rent-a-Santa Claus. Imagine walking into the local Community Center and suddenly, at the sight of 400 children, feeling transformed from a skinny, sad-eyed self, into an elf—having to chant the prescribed syllables, "Ho, Ho, Ho."

What is poetry? For me, it's the restrained music of a switchblade knife. It's an amphibious warship magically transformed into a basketball court, and then transformed again into a movie theater showing a film about the life of Joan of Arc. It is the vision of an amnesiac, bleeding from a head injury, witnessing the play of sunlight on a redbrick wall.

Poetry comes to a bearded Jewish wanderer, pulling on a pair of high rubber boots with white fur, and a set of musical sleigh bells, over blue, fleece-lined sweatpants. It comes to the father of five children bearing gifts for 400 and, choked up, unable to speak, alternately laughing and sobbing the three traditional syllables—Ho, Ho, Ho—hearing at the same time, in his heart, the more plaintive, tragic—Oi vay, Oi vay, Oi vay.

1964

Kissing
the Dancer

Uncle Dog: The Poet at 9

I did not want to be old Mr.
Garbage man, but uncle dog
who rode sitting beside him.

Uncle dog had always looked
to me to be truck-strong
wise-eyed, a cur-like Ford

Of a dog. I did not want
to be Mr. Garbage man because
all he had was cans to do.

Uncle dog sat there me-beside-him
emptying nothing. Barely even
looking from garbage side to side:

Like rich people in the backseats
of chauffeur-cars, only shaggy
in an unwagging tall-scrawny way.

Uncle dog belonged any just where
he sat, but old Mr. Garbage man
had to stop at everysingle can.

I thought. I did not want to be Mr.
Everybody calls them that first.
A dog is said, Dog! Or by name.

I would rather be called Rover
than Mr. And sit like a tough
smart mongrel beside a garbage man.

Uncle dog always went to places
unconcerned, without no hurry.
Independent like some leashless

Toot. Honorable among scavenger
can-picking dogs. And with a bitch
at every other can. And meat:

His for the barking. Oh, I wanted
to be uncle dog—sharp, high fox-
eared, cur-Ford truck-faced

With his pick of the bones.
A doing, truckman's dog
and not a simple child-dog

Nor friend to man, but an uncle
traveling, and to himself—
and a bitch at every second can

The Kite

I still heard Auntie Blue
after she did not want to come down
again. She was skypaper, way up
too high to pull down. The wind
liked her a lot, and she was lots of noise
and sky on the end of the string.
And the string jumped hard all of a sudden,
and the sky never even breathed,
but was like it always was, slow and close
faraway blue, like poor dead Uncle Blue.

Auntie Blue was gone, and I could not
think of her face. And the string fell down
slowly for a long time. I was afraid to pull it
down. Auntie Blue was in the sky,
just like God. It was not my birthday
anymore, and everybody knew, and dug
a hole, and put a stone on it
next to Uncle Blue's stone, and he died
before I was even born. And it was too bad
it was so hard to pull her down; and flowers.

Kissing the Dancer

Song is not singing,
    the snow

Dance is dancing,
    my love

On my knees, with voice
    I kiss her knees

And dance; my words are song,
    for her

I dance; I give up my words,
    learn wings instead

We fly like trees
    when they fly

To the moon. There, there are
    some now

The clouds opening, as you, as we
    are there

        Come in!

I love you, kiss your knees
      with words,

Enter you, your eyes
    your lips, like

        Lover
Of us all,

    words sweet words
    learn wings instead.

Marriage

I lie down in darkness beside her,
this earth in a wedding gown.
                    Who, what
she is, I do not know,
nor is it a question the night
would ask. I have listened—

                    The woman
beside me breathes. I kiss that,
a breath or so of her, and glow.
                    Glow.
Hush now, my shadow, let us . . .

Day breaks—

                    depart.
Yes, and so we have.

What It Was

What it was, was this: the stars
had died for the night,
      and shone;
and God, God also shone,
up, straight up, at the very
top of the sky.

        The street
was one of the better suburbs
of the night, and was a leaf,
or the color of one in the
moonlit dark.
        She, my mother,
went to the window. It was
as late as night could be
to her.
      She looked at the wind,
still, the wind,
        . . . never having blown.

And in the morning, now, of sleep
the stars, the moon and God
        began
once more, away,
        into the sky.

— And she, my mother, slept . . .
in her window, in her sky.

A Walk in the Scenery

It is there. And we are there. In it.
Walking in it, talking, holding hands.
The nickel postcard—the glossy trees;
the waterfalls, the unsuspecting
deer. A scene shot from a car window:
a slowly moving car, with many
windows, and a good camera.
And we are walking in it. We tell
ourselves, quietly, perhaps screaming,
. . . quietly, "We are walking in it."
And our voices sound, somehow, as if
we were behind windows, or within.
We embrace, and are in love. The deer
that we are watching, at the same time
(through cameras, binoculars, eyes . . .)
are so perfectly wild, and concerned
—with the scene they are, their glossy fate
silence, Nature, their rotogravure pose—
that they remain, not watching; rather,
staring away from us, into the
earnest, green and inoffensive trees.

Lost Umbrellas

She enters a room exuding displeasure,
    strewing bits of string, grievances,
    bottlecaps,
        hairnets,
    law books,
    like largess
to all corners.

From the seams of her change purse
    leak
    Travelers Cheques,
photos of used-car salesmen
    (dear brothers-in-law),
strychnine,
    ragged old horoscopes
and gifts of broken glass.

Daughter to the planet Saturn,
mother to my wife—

Her courtiers, we direct her,
mix martinis for her
find causes for her, lost umbrellas
    and car keys
even at the gates of hell.

By the Swimming

By the swimming
the sand was wetter
the farther down you dug; I dug:
my head and ear on top
of the sand, my hand felt water . . .
and the lake was blue not watching.
The water was just waiting there
in the sand, like a private lake.
And no one could kick sand
into my digging, and the water
kept going through my fingers slow
like the sand, and the sand was water too.
And then the wind was blowing everyplace,
and the sand smelled like the lake,
only wetter. It was raining then.
Everybody was making waxpaper noises,
and sandwiches, kicking sand
and running with newspapers on their heads.
Baldmen and bathinghat-ladies, and nakedpeople.
And all the sand turned brown and stuck together
hard. And the sky was lightning, and the sun
looked down sometimes to see how dark it was
and to make sure the moon wasn't there.
And then we were running: and everybody was under
the hotdog tent eating things, spitting very mad
and waiting for the sky, and to go home.

Chicago's Waldheim Cemetery

We are in Chicago's Waldheim Cemetery.
I am walking with my father.
My nose, my eyes,
    left pink wrinkled oversize
    ear
my whole face is in my armpit.

We are at the stone beneath which lies
my father's mother.
There is embedded in it a pearl-shaped portrait.
I do not know this woman.
    I never saw her.
I am suddenly enraged, indignant.
I clench my fists. I would like to strike her.
My father weeps.
He is Russian. He weeps with
    conviction, sincerity, enthusiasm.
I am attentive.
I stand there listening beside him.
After a while, a little bored,
    but moved,
I decide myself to make the effort.
I have paid strict attention.
I have listened carefully.
Now, I too will attempt tears.
    They are like song.
    They are like flight.
I fail.

"I Have Just Bought a House"

DEAR GEORGE—George, I have just bought a house,
an eighty-seven-room house. Also,
a twenty-one-room house. And many
little houses. And eighteen trailers,
and nineteen cars (six with beds in them);
and wives for all the rooms, the trailers
the little houses, and the six cars
with beds in them,
     . . . and they all love me,
all my wives love me. They do, George. They
write to me. Every day. They write
to me. And they are perfect, concise
and beautiful letters. They say—
Yes, and they say it eighty-seven times.
And then sign their names. I taught them how,
                    George,
myself. How to read and write. How to—
in houses. How to love, and how to
write perfect, concise and beautiful
letters. Yes, and how never to die.
How to live forever, for me, for
me, even though I will die. And how
to make me feel as if I won't, even
though I will, will feel as if I will.
And they are very good at it.
        Anyway,
they are all pregnant, George,
        all my wives
are pregnant. Even the parakeets.
Because some of them are parakeets.
And some are goldfish,
        silverfish, ants
rats, goats, skunks . . .
     and all have borne me children,
parakeet, silverfish, ant, rat

goldfish
children.
      And I'm happy, George. I like
marriage, really like it. Wives,
                  bedbugs
and getting mail every day.
And I feel I have a place to go.
It feels good.
      The only trouble is
I don't have any money, or even
any silverfish or rats or bedsheets
a newspaper, or a place to go.
I mean, why don't I, George?
      I live alone
in an old upright typewriter,
      with but
one dog and two cats to work
to cook, to drink beer with me.
It's sad, George. We cry ourselves
to sleep. We are so alone.
Now and then Dog sings to us—

      Woof, woof.
      Pale cats, pale man
      you shall have houses,
      you shall have wives;
      night falls

      Woof, woof.
      Beer for you, milk for you,
      sleep for you, dreams for you.

      Sleep my children,
      sleep my children,
      sleep. Woof, woof.

It is a lovely song, George,
and Dog sings it well.

We sleep.

      Witches,
nightmares big as houses, wives
warts, mushrooms,
      they are all there is.
Night-things. Things—
      pressing all the keys
around us. Wanting what? To kill us,
to put us into jail.

      Dog,
Dog barks, he barks songs at them.
They type Death onto his back,
onto his tail, his ears, his tongue.
      Fleas and lice!
We dance to avoid
the keys. We do not dance well.
We are typed into dreams, into wives.
Into mansions and swans.
      Old bedsheets, Death-sheets,
            bedbugs
      pushcarts and poems.

Scenes from a Text

"Several actual, potentially and/or really traumatic situations
are depicted on these pages."
— *Transient Personality Reactions to Acute or Special Stress*

Photo II

The house is burning. The furniture
is scattered on the lawn (tables, chairs
TV, refrigerator). Momma—
there is a small, superimposed white
arrow pointing at her—is busy
tearing out her eyes. The mute husband
(named, arrowed) stands idly by, his hands
upon his hips, eyes already out.
The smoke blankets the sky. And the scene,
apart from Momma, Poppa, the flames . . .
could be an auction. Friends, relatives
neighbors, all stand by, reaching, fighting
for the mirrors, TV, sunglasses;
the children, the cats and speechless dogs.

Emu: A Lecture for Voices; for Stereo

Three-toed, one-headed, its wings the size
of chicken-feet — and largest (next to
the ostrich) of all existing birds . . .
the emu stands, colossal, ratite
six feet high
      its god enplumaged, dark
hidden in the dismal, drooping, soft
brown hair.
    Its hips, hump, its bulge, perhaps
of flightlessness, or sky — appear as speed;
the stunted cause, the befeathered, round
sloping, still embodiment of speed.

The emu runs, swoop-skims, a two-shanked
one-humped, egg-hatched camel: the bird most
like a camel.
    Avoiding deserts
however, the emu inhabits
open fields and forests where, keeping
in small companies, it feeds on fruit
(of the emu tree), herbage and roots . . .
now and then booming, with subsequent,
and peculiarly hurried efforts,
at breeding.
    Extinct, in Tasmania
on Kangaroo, King and Wing islands,
the bird is found, and in small numbers,
in southeastern Australia.

      IT BREEDS
Its nest, as if it had been rolled in
and humped (in reverse), is a shallow
sandy, green-egg-filled pit, the eggs of which, all
nine (to thirteen), are incubated
by the cock, an earnest, familial

type of ostrich.
    The young, at birth, bear thin
length-striped down, are wattleless, and walk;
cursed, crane-necked, blank, dull adult-eyed
baby, camel, ostrich-ducks . . .
    in file
swift, point-beaked,

    mothered, three-toed, one-headed
—an image, but for the stripes (and down),
of itself, in age.

    Its booming note, god
and size, are at rest in it, in its
conspicuous state of egglessness.
It screams, booms, bounds

    . . . BECOMES IMMENSE, FLIES
extinct, shaggy, stripeless (in age)

    FLOATS
its head in the camel clouds, the hump
the bulge, the sandlessness that is God.

Attic by the River

I walk by the used river
each day
      past an old attic
(no house, the attic only
beech trees growing through it)
in a field. The river smells
of barges, rotting timbers
      water-skiers' boats, lovers
the very sun upon it.
Rivers age in Connecticut,
grow feeble, irritable
and complain like old women.
The charred attic, too,
      complains
bears ill will toward people,
      weeps
and cries, and talks aloud
on certain evenings
      to the sea.

Mothers-in-Law

Married twice now, I've had two
mothers-in-law. One visited us
and required, upon departure,
the services of three gentlemen
     with shoehorns
to get her back into her large black
Studebaker.

     The other, Momma-law the Present,
is (with the exclusion neither
     of that other,
     my wives
     nor the fathers-in-law
     of either marriage),
that Studebaker.

Nightgown, Wife's Gown

Where do people go when they go to sleep?
I envy them. I want to go there too.
I am outside of them, married to them.
Nightgown, wife's gown, women that you look at,
beside them—I knock of their shoulder blades
ask to be let in. It is forbidden.
But you're my wife, I say. There is no reply.
Arms around her, I caress her wings.

Socrates at the Symposium

SONNET FOR TWO VOICES

Of Love, my friends (after such sophistry
and praise as yours), may one presume? Well, then,
let me begin by begging Agathon:
Good sir, is not your love a love for me?
And not a love for those who disagree?
Yes, true! And what is it that Love, again,
is the love of? Speak! *It is the love again
of "Socrates."* Love then, and the Good, are me.

Explain! Is Love the love of something, or
the love of nothing? *Something!* Very true.
And Love desires the thing it loves. *Right.*
Is it, then, really me whom you adore?
Or is it nothing? *O Socrates, it's you!*
Then I am Good, and I am yours. *Agreed!*

Barbecue

—for William Dickey

I

They were spraying Pepsi and moth juice
on the fire. The mosquitoes, lawn flies
and moths dove, flashed and were painlessly
consumed. There was applause
              . . . we entered.
And while my wife was kissed, they clapped
me on the back. They wanted to know
that I was there. And then I kissed them
down their throats, choked and knew that they were there.

And after I had kissed those who had
kissed my wife, and after they kissed me,
we sprayed one another, scratched and dove
after the moths. We flashed, painlessly,
and emerged to munch the ashes, coals
to sip moth juice, lemon juice and gin.
And (again) we clapped one another
laughed, kissed, sipped, puffed and swallowed cigarettes.

II

The cat-girl would not believe in it
and crouched there pained, purring with the pups.
(Their tails were remarkably alike
and neither pronounced upon events
with them.) From time to time they'd lick one
another, or the cream dip, but otherwise
were still
      . . . though one of the pups had tried
the fire, and the cat-girl
     sleekly swallowed gin.

III
Someone found Lil, the wife of no one,
buried beside the spit. She wanted
a martini; we obliged, and then
reburied her.

Bernie dove in after the moths
only to be buried, topped, beside the spit.

IV
The sky was rainbow strips of chrome, clouds
and the sun, the great, archetypal
Ford: pork-sauced and on the suburban
spit of heaven.
        And Lil's angel waved
free, fulfilled and married now, to chrome
. . . sipping gin and tonic.
                We all stared,
climbed upon our spit, and then dove
in after the moths.
             — The fire attained to Lil.

The fire was a Ford, without chrome, pure
as gin, as cream dip, moths or spray, death
and we sang to it: its attaining
to heaven, to Lil, to space, ourselves
and the archetypal Ford.

In the other distance, in the space
the consuming that is east, the night
beyond where the moths take form, beyond
what we flash for when we die,
               we sense
the white-walled dawn, time and tomorrow's
Ford.
      There was Mars,
the suburban star of barbecue.

V

The party had somehow failed. The cards—
and there was Rummy, large as Lil, four'd
the evening star. It was time for gin
and time for light!
                         No one would admit
that he was there; we hid in front of
one another's wives. The women hid
beside the flames, the way they flickered
through their eyes. I kept trying to put my tongue

into their cards, into their eyes, ears
throats, between their teeth; but theirs were there

between mine. I bit them. And they cried
with half their tongues
                         munching diamonds and spades.

And the bushes had begun the moon,
ending "gin," martinis and marriage.

Suddenly the women screamed. The moon
burst through, revealing their husbands, the pup-girl

themselves. The bushes became the lawn;
the night, the earth; and the moths, the sun.

The men became their wives; and the wives
became the men, for the most part

remarrying themselves. The men were asleep
beside their wives, smiling, spitted, still

illicit. —Morning. My wife and I
sipped gin. I was Bernie, and she the moths.

Chicago

There are many underground things
in cities, things like sewers,
that run for miles, lengths
and widths, across cities,
under all. Then there are
the basements of large stores,
houses and hotels, and often
these basements run for twenty feet
and more out, around the buildings;
and coal, garbage and all kinds
of food are sent up and down into
the basements, or out, from the side-
walks and the alleys and streets,
by chutes, corrugated elevator
stands, iron platforms, sewertops
. . . round, rectangular or square.

And these metal things in the sidewalks,
streets, are always rather warm;
and in the winter, to comfort
and unbitter their sittings,
haunches and tails, and to avoid
the asphalt ice and cold, cats
and dogs, stray squirrels
and so forth, come at night
and from miles around, rest
and together partake.

                    And from some
distances, they and their live optic
green, brown congregations of eyes
appear as islands, still yellow
large, oval, gray or opalesque.

And no dog bites no cat, nor squirrel,
and all is quiet, idle, until the sun
comes up and chases them
out of the night, off the warmth
and good of the sewers to their parts
and tails. Then without a look
at the sun, itself, they run, trot
walking, no, no business into the snow.

All for a Day

All day I have written words.
My subject has been that: Words.
And I am wrong. And the words.
    I burn
three pages of them. Words.
And the moon, moonlight, that too
I burn. A poem remains.
But in the words, in the words,
in the fire that is now words.
I eat the words that remain,
and am eaten. By nothing,
by all that I have not made.

1965

Thousand-Year-
Old Fiancée

Hello Poem

Hello wife, hello world, hello God,
I love you. Hello certain monsters,
ghosts, office buildings, I love you. Dog,
dog-dogs, cat, cat-cats, I love you.
Hello Things-In-Themselves, Things-Not-Quite-
In-Themselves (but trying), I love you.
River-rivers, flower-flowers, clouds
and sky;
    the Trolley Museum in Maine
(with real trolleys); airplanes taking
off; airplanes not taking off; airplanes
landing,
    I love you.

The IRT,
BMT; the London subway
(yes, yes, pedants, the Underground)
system; the Moscow subway system,
all subway systems except the
Chicago subway system. Ah yes,
I love you, the Chicago El-
evated. Sexual intercourse,
hello, hello.

    Love, I love you; Death,
I love you;
    and some other things, as well,
I love you. Like what? Walt Whitman,
Wagner, Henry Miller;
    a really
extraordinary, one-legged
Tijuana whore; I love you, loved
you.

    The *Reader's Digest* (their splendid,

monthly vocabulary tests), *Life*
and *Look* . . .

      handball, volleyball, tennis;
croquet, basketball, football, Sixty-
nine;

      draft beer for a nickel; women
who will lend you money, women
who will not;

      women, pregnant women;
women who I am making pregnant;
women who I am not making pregnant.
Women. Trees, goldfish, silverfish,
coral fish, coral;

      I love you, I
love you.

Movies: Left to Right

The action runs left to right,
cavalry, the water-skiers —
then a 5-hour film, *The Sleeper*,
a man sleeping for five hours
(in fifteen sequences),
sleeping left to right, left to right
cavalry, a love scene, elephants.
Also the world goes left to right,
the moon and all the stars, sex too
and newspapers, catastrophe.

In bed, my wives are to my left.
I embrace them moving left to right.
I have lived my life that way,
growing older, moving eastward —
the speedometer, the bank balance
architecture, good music.
All that is most real moves left to right,
declares my friend the scenarist,
puffing on a white cigar, eating
The *Herald Tribune,* the *New Republic.*

My life is a vision, a mechanism
that runs from left to right. I have lived badly.
Water-skier, I was until recently
in the U.S. Cavalry. Following that
I played elephant to a lead by Tarzan.
Later, I appeared in a film called *The Sleeper.*
Till today, standing on the edge of things,
falling and about to fall asking, Why?
I look back. Nowhere. Meanwhile, one or more wives
go on stilts for the mail.

Arrival

The light goes out, the dark comes down,
small cries, low murmurs of foxes.
A light descends on the trees, whitish like what
they themselves give off. Watching it, I am moved
to prayer, to the crying out of titles
of certain poems, the names of God,
my own name. It takes shape before me.
It is the night's name, my wife's name.
In motion, in one another's arms,
we arrive somewhere where none of this is so.

At Jim McConkey's Farm

All is quiet and we lie here numbed.
There is motion, rough-winged barn swallows
and clouds. Butterflies loop around one another
suggesting bows, configurations of a knot.
Both of us lose interest. The corrugated
galvanized roof of a 100-year-old barn
refuses light. The sun comes off it
in unexpected intensities. The fields and hills
form a backdrop to this. Cicadas and song sparrows.
The landscape rolls, my eyes roll with it.
Uneasily at first, unexpectedly it comes over me
that no one will ever not love here.
The new clothespins, the look of light on the line.
Old barns. Orchards. The John Deere harvester.
I am overwhelmed by the complexities
of skunk cabbage.

       It is warmish. The breeze pleases me.
Everything is dry. We stand and walk
around in the day. We walk out to the barn
with the corrugated top. Hours later we drink beer
and ponder the hollows under stars.
I have no thoughts whatsoever. I glance at her
and embrace her, but have nothing to say.
Implausible phrases, song titles, clichés—
       they come haltingly to mind.
Then the few convictions I have done well by.
We hold hands and walk around there.
No debts. No debts. Twelve years of manuscripts.
We can go in or out. At this moment,
for this day even, we have belonged here.
How did it happen? What have we affirmed?
We kiss the one star's lips. And always, married still
      we move on.

Holding Hands

Always I am leaving people, missing them,
going out to them and loving them;
holding hands, doing turnabout, ah,
going to movies with them, clowning
reverential, an enthusiast—for what?
The certain good of sleeping with them,
holding them, climbing into their bellies.
I am present in them, approving their skins,
most foolish hopes, warmest impulses
      and the loss
of vanity, the presence of which—
and all is lost.

     Huge stars are falling,
great owls circle above us. We sit here
in wonderment—

     Is there anyone
anyone anyone has not been with?
The truth is, nothing else matters.
You are, I am, he is. The world will please
come to order. Be seated. Hold hands.
No it won't. No it won't. Don't be scared.
Cover up my love, we will all of us
never not be in you, my love love's there first.

Thousand-Year-Old Fiancée

We are alone, Death's thousand-year-old fiancée
and I. The thing suggests itself to me.
I step onto the front parts of her feet,
and stand like that facing her saying nothing.
In moments I lose twenty pounds and sweat. My nose
    bleeds.
It occurs to me I may never before
have acted out of instinct. We do not embrace.
She is in her middle sixties, with varicose veins,
whitish hair and buttocks as large as Russia.
Things come off of her in waves, merriment,
exuberance, benevolent body lice,
hundred-year-old blackheads. I kiss her hives.
I lick her nose that shows she drinks bottles
and bottles of Fleischmann's every day.
I am standing there in my Jewish hair
facing her with my life. Knock, knock.
It is Death in spats and a blue business suit.
I stand there in my Jewish hair facing him.
He is very still, grinning, grayish, bemused.
Pretty soon I begin to scream. All night I scream.

Yeah. After a while I go under and kiss
her ass. It takes a bit. Fathers and sons,
I am up to my knees in the moon.
Kiss this ghost she says of a certain light.
I plunge my tongue into it to the ears. Madam,
I say, astounded, choking, feverish,
I have not as yet had you. Have me, she says.
Under my foreskin there is a star, whole
constellations. Goddamnit, I am not
speaking to you here of sex! Kiss me here,
she says. Kiss me there. Stars, ghosts and sons,
      winged,
we are all of us wingéd—

         the one thing
there is of us. Death, you old lecher,
I affirm you, I confront you with my balls.
I revere dead fish and sunken submarines,
the little red schoolhouse and the American way.
Let us in fact join hands with the universe.
Death, I have news for you. I climb into
your young fiancée eleven times a night.
There are signs that she is pregnant.
Death, there is nothing I will not love.

People Coming out of People

Rings coming out of rings,
      four and then eight —
you reach for one, the man says,
and you have two. That is the way
rings give birth to rings. Once speaking of cups
he cried, Each is within the other,
each is linked to each. All that he did
bore witness to this. "You are pop art,"
said his woman. Marriage is like that.
What is virtue? Reach for one
and you have two. Weariness,
that is also a truth. All conditions
are truths. Claim only those
you've a mind to. All things, all truths are gifts.
The man who dreamt of playing magician
reaching for goblets, chalices, cups
one and then within it its mate,
or linked by the handles, by rims,
like women within women
the metaphysics of sex.
That too is a question —
the man reaching,
      all that he wants, doubles.
That is the way rings give birth to rings
and that is what if not a truth? (again)
cups within cups, people within people
out of love, out of need, out of want.

Halsted Street, Chicago

It is Chicago, it is Chicago
I am trying to plug in,
my finger in my navel, in Halsted Street
with holes in it; an electric light socket,
     buzz, buzz—
I want very badly to plug in.
I put my left forefinger in my ear,
and my other forefinger, I put that
exactly on the nose
     between the eyes
of Little Orphan Annie, who appears daily
     (twice daily, in fact)
on the back pages
of the *Chicago Tribune*.

I can't stand holes. I kiss people when they talk,
or put my finger in.
Also railroad tracks. I walk on them.
One day it rained. I walked for fourteen hours.
I walked all the way north to Wisconsin.
And it is true, it was good to learn:
If people see that you care for them
they do not mind your plugging in.
Coming home, no one on the bus minded
     my plugging in.
I plugged in to their buttonholes
     and shoes
     (the shoelace eyes in them).
I came back strong,
I came back with all my fingers
     and my toes too,
back once and for all now.

I unscrewed the telephone. I put my fingers in.
Click, click, the operator.
I stammered out my message, my latest coming,
deepest feelings, vibrations, revelations . . .

A failure to understand me.
Anger on my part. And a new urge to plug in.
The bent coin release, the holes in urinals,
God's left eye, heaven too, outer space
the ionosphere, the stratosphere
    the Milky Way
    and Universe in general.

Chicago Public Library

I am downtown. I am wearing sunglasses,
    phony nose,
and big inch-and-a-half-long
    false teeth.
I have them jammed on over
my other teeth.
I have the look of unabashed stupidity.
People comment on it.
Some hoodlums jeer at me,
    throw rocks at me.

It is raining. Also, it is snowing.
There are carols. It is December,
    late December,
nearly Christmas.

Old men and women are huddled in the corridor
of the Chicago Public Library.
I go there and huddle too.
I keep on my sunglasses and nose.
People like them. They admire them.
Then they look at me. They look closely,
and huddle against me. They pick my pockets,
    my pubescent blackheads,
my father's watch chain.
One of them, a dwarf, takes me by the hand.
We go walking, just the two of us.
After a while, we begin to fly.
We fly very slowly and low
and toward the lake. And then back.

I fall asleep. I have bad dreams;
I awaken—

Waldheim Jewish Cemetery,
the Outer Drive,
stainless steel florist shops,
the traffic lights,
red, amber and green.

I enter off Montrose Avenue.
Slowly, slowly
I begin the long swim
      to Michigan.

Satires

The New York Times Book Review

Sunday, March 18, 1962

This critic in bed with this poet,
in bed with this female writer
    of scenarios,
O General X, O General Y,
    beneath the bed,
but in it nonetheless,
    Dr. Spock,
Dr. Edward Teller, proud father
of the H-bomb, I see you there . . .
you are there too, reviewed by RAND,
planting mushrooms in the chamber pot.

    O Dr. Strontium, O Folk Medicine
    encyclopedias of saleable wars,
    picture books of extinct everything,
    aphrodisiacs, erotica —

Historians embracing historians,
novelists embracing novelists,
their hands in one another's crotches,
pens in one another's pockets;
    books
in one another's books.

    O hold me,
hold me close, I want to sleep there too,
where the warmth is, where the money is,
    aura
of martinis. Reserve a bit of sheet
for me, I want in, I want in
with the New English Translation
of the Bible, Writers' Workshop teachers
O and all the others of America's
O charming, honey-fingered men of letters.

American Heritage

This, O my stomach, is a painting
of the Civil War. Look—Antietam.
All over there are dead,
noble Northern, noble Southern, dead.
One, no, no, several wear beards.
They are all General Ulysses Grant beards,
noble, truly noble beards.
The Union side, O my soul, see them!
All, all of them waving,
resembling, bearing the name
Walt Whitman. They are all on horseback,
all with maps and swords, banners
and copies of last Sunday's
New York Times Book Review
watching through binoculars,
writing letters, keeping journals,
reading *Leaves of Grass* . . .

And there is Barbara Fritchie.
Hi, Barbara. Barbara's pregnant.
She is soon to be the mother
of Abraham Lincoln, Dr. Oliver Wendell Holmes
and Carl Sandburg.

This is a historical moment,
very historical. You can feel it
and read about it, too
(and General Stonewall Jackson,
Clare Boothe Luce, Robert E. Lee
        and many others),
in *American Heritage,*
edited by Bruce Catton,
with whose kind permission
I herewith reprint this painting.

   * * *

Song: "There's No War Like Civil War"

O the Civil War's
the only war,
the only war, the only war;
the finest war,
yes, the noblest most unforeign war,
the finest only noblest most
unforeign war
that ever I did see. (Chorus, etc.)

"Suds" in Terrycloth — Mr. & Mrs.

Ahh, froths she, her soapchip teeth
to Mr. Terry S.

She like he is in her "clean clear through"
(and deodored, too!) bathrobe.

Raising her FAB right arm, one hand
against the armpit

And the other at her wrist, he gnaws
and drools into the terrycloth.

Ahh, cries she, her teeth and tongue
at him. She seems pleased.

He grins and glistens from his eyes.
He licks her then, up

And down her spine, Ahh!
licked-lipped, she runs her tongue . . .

"Dazzling white (to be sure), but
something more. It's as if

"Suds and sunlight had combined
to Terry swiftly, agilely through

"And up and down her robe. No wonder he
can't keep his tongue away!"

Ahh! Its thick, soft white nap
outdates all dulling soapscum cleanliness.

Nor is his robe without its attractions.
She sniffs his bushy belt. He reddens,

Froths into the air, and slaps
his little webbed feet hard upon the floor.

She spreads her robe to him; and he, his
to her. She moistens him

And he, her. Bursting from within their pelts,
teeth bubbles suds, ahh—

"The Very Air He Breathes"

She lies upon a tawny mat
of effluence — and leopard spots.

And he *(he's hers*
and she knows it!)

Can but barely be seen, crouched
and to the left of her.

One ear, an eyebrow, and a bit of cheek
are all that show of him.

The caption (again) suggests that it is fun
(fabulous fun) being female

At a time like this!
And, indeed, it looks like fun.

Her eyes are huge and subtly closed
as leopard spots; and her lips are spread.

She is, in fact, a deodored leopardess
about to take the male.

But again, the caption: *You are the very air*
he breathes (the male is hard upon her).

She appears to be undisturbed by this;
and with both shaved armpits bared, she arches

For him. One is inclined to think of her
as being altogether without fear; she smiles,

And takes the male. Neither deodorant,
nor effluence, could do more.

                    She smiles,
and she lies there, the very air
he breathed.

Nine-and-a-Half Times

They had killed Momma's brother Johnny
nine-and-a-half times in the war. There
wasn't hardly anything left when
he got home: of Johnny or of Momma.
I mean he came home without his arms,
without his ears, without his brains, or
hair; without his loving everyone,
     and women
That made Momma mad. He didn't like
love no more, or Momma, and he had
been married in between all the times
he was killed. Nine-and-a-half times!
And Momma had cried and cried and said
it was like his being killed. The Army
and President Roosevelt, General
Eisenhower . . .
     They were all sorry,
and Momma ate the letters and the envelopes;
the telegrams, and then Johnny; the Purple
Heart, the White Heart, the gold
star, Daddy & all of Johnny's wives.
And Momma was all that there was left.

Report from the Front

All over newspapers have stopped appearing,
and combatants everywhere are returning home.
No one knows what is happening.
The generals are on long distance with the president,
a former feature writer for the *New York Times*.
No one knows even who has died, or how,
or who won last night, anything.
Those in attendance on them may,
for all we know, still be there.
A few speak compulsively, telling too much,
having sat asleep in easy chairs.

All over newspapers have stopped appearing.
Words once more, more than ever,
have begun to matter. And people are writing
poetry. Opposing regiments, declares a friend of mine,
are refusing evacuation, are engaged instead
in sonnet sequences; though they understand, he says,
the futility of iambics in the modern world.
That they are concerned with the history and meaning
of prosody. That they persist in their exercises
with great humility and reverence.

1975

Five Iowa Poems

Iowa City, Iowa

"Some years the ground pulls harder —"

He mounts his tractor.
There are creatures in trees
whose names I do not know.
There are others in procession before us.
Pigs the size of buffalo. Cattle
the tails and markings of horses.
Iowa. What am I doing in Iowa?
Ann lies in the sun. Dozing. Depressed.
Stripping, rising on my hind legs,
hairy, cloven-footed,
Centaur, I declare myself: Centaur.
Then chicken. Then horse. Bull. Then pig.
She too: Centaur. Then chicken. Horse. Bull. Then pig.
Let us plant our dreams.
Write them down and plant them.
Plant sugar cubes.
Make love.
Then dig it up, turn it over
and plant the ground,
that ground we made love on.
What will grow there?
Rhubarb.
A peach tree.
The ground holds me as I make love to it.
How is it birds no longer fly?
Horses only. The entire state of Iowa.
What about deities,
these deities that eat your brains?
And why anyway should I mind that?
I am busy planting my brains.
I will harvest them remind me please before leaving.
The time has come.
O look Centaur   Snowing   Your eyes
your eyes

they touch me.
I have been asleep.

Does it hurt?

Iowa

What a strange happiness.
Sixty poets have gone off drunken, weeping into the hills,
I among them.
There is no one of us who is not a fool.
What is to be found there?
What is the point in this?
Someone scrawls six lines and says them.
What a strange happiness.

Iowa Writers' Workshop — 1958

—for Paul Engle

Seated, against the room, against the walls
legs extended, or under chairs
iambs, trochees & knees . . .
we surrender, each of us, to the sheets
at hand. The author swallows his voice. Still

"Page two." Page one is saved for the last.
"The poet has here been impressed
by the relationship
between blue birds and black. In the octet
we note the crow. And its iambic death."

"On page three, *The Poet upon His Wife*
(by his wife), we note the symbols
for the poet: the bird
in flight, the collapsing crow, the blue bird . . .
Note too the resemblance between sonnets."

We vote and stare at one another's crow.
Ours is an age of light. Our crows
reflect the age, Eisenhower-Nixon
colored stripes, rainbow-solids, blacks & whites.
Ruffling their wings, Mezey, Coulette, Levine
    refuse to vote.

"Page four, *Apologies to William S.*
apologies, our third sonnet . . ."
And those who teach, who write
and teach, the man at hand, apologize
for themselves, and themselves at hand.

"Poets buy their socks at Brooks & Warren,
like DuPont, like Edsel, like Ike."
Anecdotes, whispers, cliques
whispering, then aloud into prominence.
Brooks & Warren, DuPont, Edsel & Ike.

Order is resumed. *"We have been here, now
forever. From the beginning
of verse."* One has written
nothing, and it is inconceivable
that one would, or will ever write again.

A class has ended. They pass by, gazing
in. The poets gaze out, and grin.
They gaze out, and through the
electric voice, the ruffled sonnet sheets
that stare against the faces staring in.

"Page one." Walled-in glances at the author.
And then the author disappears,
the poem anonymous.
Voice. Voices. There are voices about it:
anonymous. The self. A sonnet's self . . .

The room is filled with it. It is a bird.
It sits beside us and extends
its wings. Mezey hits it with his elbow.
The bird shrieks and sprawls
upon the floor. We surrender

We surrender to its death. The poem breathes,
becomes its author and departs.
We all depart. And watch
the green walls take our seats. Apologies.
Brooks & Warren. DuPont. Edsel & Ford.

Impossible Hurricane Loss-of-Name Poem

The fields planted.
Tractors   Wooden clothespins rising.
Parched. Brown. Plows and houses. Rising.
Rainbow. It ends or begins or starts.
Is it walking or is it skipping?
It rides above the fence.
If I dig a hole will I find a poem?
A pot of unicorns?
A herd of leprechauns?
I ask. The rainbow has already moved.
Seven miles in the soft light.
A field filled with cows.
The hurricane approaches.
There are funnels filled with butterflies.
Dust that is the rain.
Thunder. Trees. The grass.
The wind walking.
Phosphorous. The rain.
The noiseless. Wind. Explodes.
I am lying in the sun only there is none.
I am being blown away   only
the moon rises   which
is the sun? Evening. There is none.
Red. Parched brown. Plows and houses.
Hurricane. Hurricane.
My name has been blown away.
O name poor name,
will the rain care for you as I have cared for you?
Will the wind devour you,
knock your head against a tree?
Already I have forgotten.
Can a young man named . . .
live happily in a hurricane?
Will his house and woman and poems blow away?
Once they have blown away. Twice. Already.

That the house and the woman and the unnamed man
have their tongues in one another's mouths,
can they go on like that?
Funnel, stars, butterfly,
wind. The noiseless
Yes, they can.

1978

**Honey Bear on
Lasqueti Island,
B.C.**

Honey Bear

She is a Russian honey bear
with very strong soft brown arms.
Hugging her is at once a feat
of strength, and an act of gentle surrender.

One cannot hug the honey bear
with only half a heart. It's all
or no honey bear. There's a snap
and vibrancy to her kisses

Pucker and snap—audible
across a field of wild black
berries. Honey bear loves fresh cream
and wild berries of all kinds

French cheeses and homebaked bread.
She is earth tremors in the garden,
laughter in the flower beds
rough brown honey bear pulling weeds.

Her feet, large, perfectly
        proportioned
        are powerful as
angel wings. A pale blue light
surrounds her toes as she waltzes

By the clover and the mint.
Lighter than air, heavier
than a bear. Clear-skinned lady
O fairest of the fair

I bow to my honey bear.

Bear Mother

    Mystery.
Familiarity. Moving together
of bodies. The dance of mouths,
hands, bellies and tongues lightly touching
    knees and hairs and milky toes.

        *   *   *

Black bear mother with magic eyes
and dancing feet
crouching, squatting
giving birth
dropping a single cub
the cub grunting, sticky,
moaning.

Bear Mother in the Kaleidoscope

Her lips are kindly and full.
Her eyes are blue,
mouth like pale cherries
     ripe on trees
     with snow.

She appears without clothes
     or fur
in a white velvet tent
on an enchanted island.
She's a white hummingbird
at the float house
in the evening
circling clockwise
round the fire.

     *   *   *

Dark goes into light.
Dark is a black cord on a silver needle
drawn by a bear
through a cave
     shining
     glistening
in the dripping darkness
reflecting fire.

     *   *   *

In our boat at night —
with herself as passenger —
we navigate
     over rocks,
submerged, undiscovered islands,
moons like gigantic human eyes,

lunar gardens and small mansions,
wooden houses
    floating
    in the sea.

Gull, Clam — Wham

Gull flies up in the air
with a clam
drops it on the rocks
crack, bam, wham goes the clam

And, as it doesn't open,
gull flies up with it again.
And again drops it
    on the rocks
plop, bop, and wham again.

This time the clam opens and the gull
feasts. Gull flies up the channel
from west to east,
then back again down the same channel.

Hot summer's day.
Sun coming down.
A little breeze, out on the rocks
crack, bam, wham
    goes the clam

While we in our float house
lean out, looking to the east
and the mud flats filled with clams.
Walking out with shovels, digging
    for clams.

Gulls to the east of us
gulls to the west
gulls, gulls, clam bam wham
gulls, gulls, wham bam clam.

Clambake, clambake
get yourself a clam to bake.

Clambake, clambake
crack, bam, wham goes the clam.

Clambake, clambake
gull, clam — wham.
Clambake, clambake
gull, clam — wham.

Float House Cooking—Written While
Sloshed on Lasqueti Island, B.C.

—for Maureen & Jerry Curle

Standing up to the knees
in water, he squeezes
a little lemon onto
the vegetables being sautéed

In butter on a wok
as he stands in water
in front of a Coleman stove
resting on a rock.

The rice is steaming
and the tea is brewing
the oysters are stewing
and about cooking like this
      there is no fooling

Around, silly as it may be
standing in up to the knees
pressing the garlic, opening
      the teas
being knocked over by the tide,

The main hazard of cooking
on a float house. O friends,
forgive the cook if, eating
and enjoying this dish, you feel

A little seasick or uneasy
queasy in the tummy.
Be assured, dear hungry friends,
it is not my cooking

And it is no blow to my pride
to freely admit the saltiness
of the rice is owing

    to its falling into the sea
because of the tide, you see —
not me.

For My Son, Michael

Lasqueti Island, B.C.

Washing dishes in the darkness
with a hose,
I spray off the few
        remnants
of spaghetti onto the oysters

In their beds below.
Inside the single room
there is no running water —
        only the green hose
on the deck of our floating home.

We secure the lines,
bathe and sing.
I reach out in the darkness
hearing my son brushing his teeth
to borrow his toothbrush.

I cannot find my own:
it is tasting
        my fourteen-year-old son's
mouth inside my mouth.
Then we find more dishes

And, as the moon rises and the lines
        go tight,
continue scrubbing and drying silverware
and plates,
        two dishwashers reading braille,
        mad beachcombers in the night.

1983

Movies:
Left to Right

Blind Poet

—for Marcie

She has braces on her teeth and wears
a blue and orange plaid cotton shirt:

One of fourteen students

Wiggles, chatters, finds her way
into her friends' poems.

Straightens her back like a pianist
readying herself for a performance.

Sitting upright, intent
she completes, aloud,
ahead of the others

Their own, half-formed images. "Damnit, Marcie,
whose poem is this?"

They squirm, they squabble, and defer.
Composing herself,
both hands moving smoothly

Over an embossed braille keyboard
of otherwise blank pages,
she reads

From a manuscript of dots. First
a lyric
she has just written

And hastily transcribed—before class—
and another,
"Wishing You Were Here."

Like a passenger waking
aboard a crowded ferryboat
on a frozen lake

My voice
lost in the voices
of the others, I cry out

"Hey, you prodigy
ferryboat captain,
inventor in the night,

"Who's writing this anyway?"

Mr. Amnesia

Even an amnesiac remembers some things
    better than others.
In one past life I was a subway conductor
for the Chicago subway system.

In another I was — Gosh, I forgot!
Anyway, some years ago, I was run over
by a sports car. Ever since that time

I find I cannot go more than a few days
without leaving my body at least briefly
and then coming back to it. Again and again.

I can't seem to stay in Chicago or in any city,
for that matter, and in one body,
for very long.

I once wrote a forty-nine-line poem
made up entirely of first lines, forty-nine beginnings.
"Forty-Nine Beginnings" it was called.

I once met a young mother who had gone fishing
with her two children. Coming up from the bottom
of Lake Michigan, I got tangled up in their lines

And they pulled me out and saved my life.
The woman was my wife and the children were
    my children.
"Making love, it's always as if it were happening

"For the first time," I said after ten years of marriage.
"When a woman chooses an amnesiac as her husband,
she has to expect things like that," she laughed.

"Still, there's a lot to be said
for ten years of foreplay."
An Instructor in Modern Poetry, I once lectured

For four weeks as if each class was the first class
of a new year. When the genial chairman,
manifesting polite alarm,

Visited my classes, the occasion of his being there
gave me the opportunity to teach
as if those classes, too, were new classes.

Promoted, given a raise, a bonus and a new two-year
                    contract,
even I was confused. Each class I taught became one
in an infinite series of semesters, each semester

Lasting no more than fifty minutes.
I don't know about you, but I hardly unpack
and get ready for this lifetime and it's time

To move on to the next. I've been reincarnated
                    three times,
and am forty-nine years old and I don't even know
                    my own name.
History is just one of those things

You learn to live without. I live in a city
the entire population of which is made up of amnesiacs
so for the first time in three lifetimes I feel at home.

Yaddo

I'm at Yaddo sheltering myself from the drizzle
    standing under a tree
reading Philip Roth's *The Great American Novel*
waiting for my friends Joe and Carol Bruchac
to arrive
with four friends from Canada
who are in Saratoga Springs, New York,
to give a poetry reading,
Bruce Meyer, Richard Harrison, Robert Lawrence
    and Ross Leckie,
when up pulls this big shiny car
which I approach smiling
thinking it's Joe and Carol,
but it's not, it's Burns International
    Security Services, Inc.
and the man wants to know if Yaddo
has anything more than "internal security."
    "I'm John Weidman," he says.
"You must be a writer."
"Yep."
"What's your name?"
"Sward, my name is Robert Sward, like greensward."
"Oh," he says, disappointed he doesn't
know any of my books but
still impressed to be meeting
a Yaddo author.
I should have said, "My name is
Philip Roth, John, and this is my new book,
    The Great American Novel,
but as usual I think of things like that
    too late.
"Look," he says, handing me his business card,
    J. W. Weidman
    Security Sales Consultant,
"Mention my name in your next book, okay?"

Personal Stress Assessment
(FOUND POEM)

> "Make a list of all the life events that apply to you . . . then add
> them up with the points assigned."

To be married and moderately unhappy
is less stressful than to be unmarried
and male and over 30.
To be happily married counts for 0 points.
If your spouse dies that counts for 100 points.
63 for going to jail. 73 for divorce.
Divorce is more stressful than imprisonment.
Getting married is 3 points more stressful
than being fired. Marital reconciliation (45 points)
and retirement (also 45 points)
are only half as stressful as
the death of your spouse.
Minor violations of the law: 11 points.
Trouble with the boss: 23. Christmas: 12. But
sexual difficulties are less stressful
than pregnancy (40 points versus 39).
A mortgage over $10,000 is worse
than a son (or daughter) leaving home.
Trouble with your in-laws is as stressful
as "outstanding personal achievement"
which is only slightly more stressful
than if "wife begins or stops work."

Are you very happy and well adjusted? 0 points.
Very angry, depressed or frustrated? 20 points.

Conclusion: With 25 points or more, "you probably
will feel better if you reduce your stress."

1983

Half-a-Life's
History

Half-a-Life's History

(EXCERPTED FROM *THE JURASSIC SHALES*)

Scenario: An amnesiac wakes one morning in
London, England, in bed with two women. In the
process of recovering his memory, he goes back in
time 160 million years to the Jurassic geological
period to find his true original parents, the first
of the flying dinosaurs. The narrator is himself
a flying dinosaur, and *The Jurassic Shales* ends
with his being united with his father and mother.

Here I am writing to you
half-a-life's history
"A horse which throws the dreamer to the ground."
I am homesick and America has had a nervous breakdown.
I am taking shaman lessons and studying karate.
My greatest complaint (you've offered to help) is amnesia.
Do you believe in transmigration of the soul? Yes, I do too.
But what if it can happen not only when one dies, but
        several times in an afternoon?
And I'm sure it's not properly amnesia I am speaking of.
I go out of my body, I come back in.
I say amnesia because sometimes when this happens
        I forget just who I am.
I've been doing this, I believe, with some regularity for
        a quarter of a million years. I'm doing it more
        and more frequently now because I'm unhappy.
        Even the light depresses me. That is, the light
        on Oxford Street, 6 PM on a Sunday. The light
        in Bloom's. The light in Wimpy's. I haven't seen
        light like this since the Middle Ages of the Animals.

We drink, we smoke, we go to parties. Friday night
        we went to the dullest party in 3,000 years
        in Bayswater off the Moscow Road.

I thought the whole time of algae, worms,
      primitive brachiopods, molluscs, crustaceans,
I thought of my mother and those birds with the hollow
      bones.
I am in the library at Swiss Cottage
      eating chocolates in the children's room
What am I reading? Probably I have gone mad.
I am reading up on the eohippus, the first true
      archaic horse.
I identify. Those horses were no larger than dogs.
      I'm a dog and interested in horses
that were once my own size.
Why? I don't know why. Yes, I do. It's because
      I feel I was once (also) a wooly rhinoceros.
That I am at this moment a wooly rhinoceros. .
Anyway, I am no longer incapacitated by my erotic
      fantasies.
I am devoting my whole attention to insects, geology, etc.
Each morning I have friends come in to read me my
      biography and my passport.
Then I know who I am. Then I can pay attention
      to what needs to be done.

Who are these people anyway? They think they speak English,
      but I don't understand a word they say.
My only reason for coming was to learn karate with Kanazawa,
      who has left for Germany.
Oh, I've just gone out of my body and now I'm back.
What is happening in America where, I am convinced,
      in my previous existence, I was a Confederate
      soldier killed in action, 186-?
Well, it doesn't matter. I'll find out soon enough and probably
      know anyway if I'd only think about it.

Before I was born, my mother who is the Mother of fire,
      gave birth to fire. Then to the Sabine women
      and my sister.

My father, who has an upright tail, practices and earns his living
    in Chicago. That he is a Rosicrucian and I am not
is no obstacle. We have made our peace, and increasingly—
I might say this is a love poem for my father. A love poem for
    the seven maidens with the heads of snakes.
Half-a-life's history.

Returning to Live in 1860

Good morning, 1860.
Good morning.
Good morning, Dr. Whimsy.
Good morning.
Good morning, Beauty.
Truth.
Queen.
Helicopter karma machine.
Industry.
Business machines. Computers.
Simplicity.
Can I have just an hour with the milkmaid?
I want to get back right away then to waging
     the Civil War.
What instructions are there?
Has the queen left a note? Can I play Lord Shepperton's
     harmonica?
Women being mediums for all I know and for all
     I will ever know (How can I know that, how
     can I assign myself—?)
I want another hour with the milkmaid and the queen
     to read me her diaries and to instruct me
     in every extreme action of which she knows anything.
I want to know the bounds of things and sense,
     and how to cleanse myself.

Is there any peanut butter?
What incredible sticky things are there to eat
     this century?
When did they invent ice cream?
Anyone carrying on like this is carrying on
     for a reason.
What is the reason?
Where is the child?

But perhaps being forty years before them, I can
    become both my parents' parents.
Has that been done before?
And what if they've gone back forty or even
    sixty years.
What if they're at this moment in the process
    of becoming their own parents?
When will they get to me? When will it be my turn?
I'd like to be present and film my own birth,
to come out with a camera and to be obstetrician,
    my waiting father and director
    at the same time.
I'd like in fact to be my mother, giving birth
    to an obstetrician-director-my-waiting-
    father and a movie camera.
And to come out with on my wrist
a wrist-sized washing machine, etc., so I could be
    immediately fully independent. A stove. Hi-fi.
    A library. A hospital with my own
    doctors. And a complete set of in-laws.
The question most on my mind:
Where do women come from?
Women come right out of the head of the male god.
Either that or out of the earth—or things about
the earth. People here, there, everywhere, both
ears against it. Listen. Everybody. Alright,
we're listening.

Who are these women with?
Where do they come from?
How do they get that way?

The bride is with—
the queen is with—
What about Cassandra? What about Hera?
Are things complementary in more ways even
    than one suspected?
When what happens and what you do

are the same thing
how is it possible to speak of loving someone or
     wasting time?

I want a banana. I want a tangerine.
I want to rim the most beautiful woman in Manhattan,
     Kansas.
What about Jesus Christ? Where is there a tape
     of him laughing?
In sex, I've found, in loving
the discovery is the cleansing.
I want to swallow it down.
The only sadness is loving
AND NO ILLUMINATION.
Beauty is wallowing.
Loving is practice.
A man having been with a woman, the woman has
     always been there.
Has the man always been there?

from Scarf Gobble Wallow Inventory

How hungry and for what are the people this season
     predicting the end of the end of the end of
I've only just come home after having been away
The world sends its greetings and the greetings
     send greetings
Hello goodbye, hello goodbye
There are greetings and gifts everywhere
Children screaming and feeling slighted
The next minute we're walking along canals
     on the planet Mars
Twenty minutes later we are earthworms in black
     leather jackets, our pockets filled
     with hamburgers,
Voyage to the moon.
All I am really hungry for is everything
The ability to hibernate and a red suitcase going off
     everywhere
Every cell in your body and every cell in my body is
     hungry and each has its own stomach
Are your cells eating my cells? Whose cell is the
     universe, and what is it sick with, if anything?
Is the universe a womb or a mouth?
And what is hunger, really?
And is the end of the world to be understood in terms of
     hunger or gifts, or the tops of peoples' heads
     coming off?
The most complex dream I've ever dreamed I dreamed
     in London.
It involved in its entirety taking one bite of an orange.

       ★   ★   ★

"What do you want to be when you grow up?" she says.
I'm nearly sixty.
I want to be hungry as I am now and a pediatrician.

The truth is I'm 45 and hungrier than I was when I was
    20 and a sailor.
I'm hungry for ice cream made with ice cream and not
    chemicals or artificial spoons.
I've never been so hungry in my life.
I want one more bacon-lettuce-and-tomato
    sandwich,
to make love and kiss everyone I know goodbye.
Tomorrow at half past four we will all four-and-a-half
    billion of us walk slowly into orbit.
If only one can do this breathing normally, and not trip
    on one's breath or have stomach cramps or clammy
    hands or hysterical needs or a coughing fit or the wish
    to trample or stomp someone, but stepping peacefully
There is ALL the time in the world
There is ALL THE TIME IN THE WORLD
There is all the time in the world.

Statement of Poetics, or
"Goodbye to Myself"

I wrote for myself
for people. I've
changed.
I've changed since I
began writing *I write
for myself.* I believe
more than ever in
music, in the sound,
however gotten, of music
in people's poetry. Rhyme
more than ever. Talk
people talking, getting that
into one's poetry that
is my poetics. Love
hate lies laughing stealings
self-confession, self-destruction
get them all get
them all down.
No one has to
read them. No one
has to publish them.
I am more and
more for unpublished poetry.
That is why I
have a pseudonym that
is why I now
publish poetry. To control
the view.
To hell with the Business
of Anthologies. To hell
with Anthologies.

To hell too with the way I
taught poetry in the

1950s, 1960s and 1970s.
One way and another
I have written angry poetry for
twenty years. Now I
want music only and
the sounds of people.
I want poems
that sing
and can use
the word *heart* and
self-confession and incorrect
grammar and the soils
and stains of Neruda
and Lorca and Kabir
and Williams and
Whitman and Yeats.

Forty-four years old.
Stands on his head
ten minutes daily morning
breakfast, supper.
Writing less and less.
Evaporating into the air
feet first. I won't
ever die. I'll simply
stand on my head
and disappear into the
air just like that.

I don't believe in
imagination. The prairies
as a landscape
are imagination. Just as
England is, as a landscape,
a failure of imagination.
Africa is imagination, India
is reaching even further
than that. And that

is why I will
go to India which
I will in seven
days' time. So this
is a time capsule
in case anyone is
interested and in case
I never come back.
This is a
statement of poetics written
as "Goodbye to myself."

Goodbye for
now, goodbye
goodbye goodbye
to myself,
goodbye goodbye
for now
goodbye myself,
goodbye for
now goodbye.

1985

Poet Santa Cruz

A Monk on the Santa Cruz Mountains

—after Ts'en Ts'an

They say there is a monk on the Santa Cruz Mountains,
his white robes floating, three hundred feet beneath
    the sky.
A barefoot, thousand-year-old,
    chocolate-colored genie
who has not spoken in three lifetimes.
His matted, ankle-length hair housed
    a family of scorpions.
Now, small children approach him, dance
and whirl about with his walking stick
which once separated
two demons in a death struggle.

Castroville, California — A Coffee Shop cum Art Gallery in the Artichoke Capitol of the World

Sonnet

O thistle-like artichoke in the place
of glory. Green peppers: four lushly framed nudes
staring down on us with a kind of greasy grace.
Purple and green eggplants like immodest prudes.

And apples of heroic size, left to right
like paintings of smugly pompous ancestors.
Broccoli plus pale mushrooms in the moonlight,
whitely bulbous omniscient lecturers

On the care and curatorship of fruit
and vegetables which play more a part
in our lives than the sad-eyed, ruling dupes
who clutter up our walls displacing fruits.

I never did before, but now I will:
I sing, dear friends, of brave plain Castroville.

Li Po (circa A.D. 701-762)

—after Robert Payne's *The White Pony*

Tall, powerfully built with a loud screeching voice
and bright, hungry tigerish eyes, his black hair
flowing over his shoulders.
The high heavenly priest of the white lake
with murderers and thieves for ancestors.
Musician, swordsman and connoisseur of fine wines,
      a drunk, a murderer—
Mr. Fairyland, Mr. Landscape of an
      impossible flowering.
He was called a god in exile, the great phoenix
whose wings obscure the sun.
"I am strong enough," boasted this poet, "to meet
ten thousand men."

Li Po who, at death, was summoned by angelic hosts,
who rode off on the backs of dolphins
and, led by the two children of immortality,
entered the celestial palace in triumph.

The Emperor

A Villanelle

From *The Way and Its Power*

The world as seen in vision has no name;
call it the Sameness or the Mystery
or rather the "Darker than any Mystery."

Fan Li who, offered half a kingdom,
stepped into a light boat and was heard from
no more. The world as seen in vision has no name.

An empty vessel that one draws from
without its ever needing to be filled. The name-
less, the darker than any Mystery.

Can you love people, rule the land,
yet remain unknown? Play always the female part?
The world as seen in vision has no name.

Rear them, feed them, but do not lay claim.
He who in dealing with the empire,
darker than any mystery,

Regards his high rank as though it were
his body, is the best person to be entrusted with rule.
The world as seen in vision has no name;
call it the Darker than any Mystery.

New Releases

Clancy the Dog

—for Claire

He is so ugly he is a psalm to ugliness,
this extraterrestrial, shorthaired
midget sea lion,
snorts, farts, grunts, turns somersaults
on his mistress's bed.

She calls him an imperfect Boston terrier,
part gnome, part elf,
half something and half something else,
180,000,000-year-old Clancy
with his yellowy-white, pin-pointy teeth
and red, misshapen prehistoric gums.

Clancy has no tail at all and doesn't bark.
He squeaks like a monkey,
flies through the air,
lands at six every morning
on his mistress's head,
begging to be fed and wrapped not in a robe
but a spread.

Tree frog, warthog, groundhog,
"Clancy, Clancy," she calls for him
in the early morning fog,
and he appears, anything, anything,
part anything but a dog.

Scarlet the Parrot

Scarlet perches on the office windowsill
shrieking, hollering, barking

Like a dog. She knocks her mottled beak
against the warehouse window

And tries to open
the metal hook-and-eye latch.

There are parrot droppings
on the telephone and Scarlet has eaten

Part of the plastic receiver.
The parrot slides like a red fireman

With yellow and blue feathers
up and down the cord,
        holding on

With her beak, maneuvering gracefully
        with her claws.
When I approach she calls, "Hello, hello .

Walks up my trouser leg holding on
with her macaw's beak. I feed the bird

Oranges and pears, almonds
and sunflower seeds.

I swivel my head round and round
in imitation of her neck movements.

"What's happening?" she asks,
and again, "What's happening?"

"Hello, cookie. Yoo-hoo . . .
Can you talk, can you talk?" she asks

Chewing for several minutes,
finally swallowing
         a leather button

Off my green corduroy jacket, threatening,
ready to tear my ear off,

Biting if I place my finger
in her mouth. Her tongue is black

And her beady eyes piercing like an eagle's.
She wants a response, tests my reactions.

Tenderly the parrot walks up my corduroy jacket,
sensually restraining her claws. I'm aroused.

When a dog barks, she barks too: Rrf, rrf.
Casually, a relaxed but authentic

Imitation. "Hello, darling," she breathes,
looking me in the eye knowing I know

If it pleases her she might bite my ear off.
"Yoo-hoo, yoo-hoo, now you say something," she says.

Alfa the Dog

It isn't enough that when I go off for three weeks to an
artists' colony and phone home the first thing my wife
tells me is there's a new addition to the family, a seven-
month-old poodle named Alfa and that Alfa has papers,
an honest-to-God pedigree that includes not only aristo-
cratic ancestors, but recent appearances in the *New York
Review of Books* and a novel published by Houghton-
Mifflin. And when I am somewhat less than ecstatic,
my wife asks me to at least say a few words to the new
addition, and puts on Alfa the dog. "Speak, Alfa, speak,"
I hear her say. And Alfa who is, by all accounts, loyal
and obedient, a noted storyteller, intelligent and amusing
as Oscar Wilde, refuses to speak, to bark, or make some
witty remark like, "What's the weather like in Saratoga?"
All I hear is Alfa's low doggy breathing and the tinkle
of the elegant silver bell on her collar.

My wife comes back on and says, "I have an idea. You
bark into the phone. Alfa will answer back."

Well, it's only costing a dollar ninety-five a minute and
good-natured soul that I am, devoted to my wife, guilty
at running off for three weeks, I put myself into it, throw
back my head and howl, barking, yowling, yipping like a
real dog—a dog without papers, a dog with fleas, a dog
like one of those mutts I knew growing up in Chicago,
and this happening, of course, on the public pay phone
at Yaddo, the "artists' heaven," what the *New York Times*
calls the Harvard of Artists' Colonies.

Looking up, sure enough, I see one of America's more
distinguished composers with his mouth open, his pipe
falling to the floor, waiting in line, no doubt, to speak
to his wife and children and his cats and dogs.

"Well, darling," I say, "we've been talking for twenty-five minutes. This is going to cost a fortune."

At that moment, Alfa decides she wants to make her presence known to all concerned, and she begins barking into the phone, answering me in kind, responding yip for yip, and yap for yap, lest there be any doubt in anyone's mind as to who it is I have been speaking, me to Alfa the dog, Alfa the dog to me.

Three Roberts

From heart to heart
from brain to brain
from Robert to Robert

Robert Zend phones Robert
Sward. *Ring, ring.*
"Robert, this is Robert."

"Is this Robert?" "This
is Robert, Robert." "Yes,
Robert?" I say. "This

"Is Robert, too." "Ah,
excuse me, I need
to find a match,"

Says Robert Zend putting
down the telephone
and rummaging for matches,

Granting me, a nonsmoker,
the status of accessory
to his addiction.

All this occurring a few
seconds into an otherwise
scintillating conversation.

"I had a very pleasant afternoon
while reading your poems,"
Margaret Trudeau once remarked

About Zend's book, *From Zero to One,*
and I can fully understand
her saying that.

Zend translates serious things
into funny things
and funny things

Into serious things.
He also translates himself
into other people, and

Other people into himself—
and where does one of us end
and the other begin?

And where does Zend begin
and where do I zend?
I mean, end?

And what about Robert Priest?
Is he a visible man,
an invisible man?

Or the man who broke out of the Letter X?
Is he a spaceman in disguise?
A blue pyramid? A golden trumpet?

A chocolate lawnmower?
An inexhaustible flower?
Or a reader who escaped

From some interstellar library?
Rock Musician in residence
at the University of the Moon?

And meanwhile Robert Zend
looks into his mirror
and sees not Zend

But Chicago-born Uncle Dog;
Half-a-Life's History;
Mr. Amnesia; Mr. Movies: Left to Right;

Mr. Transmigration of the Soul;
the poet as wanderer;
a forty-nine-year-old human violin . . .

Robert Zend the Nomad
gazing in like an acrobat
at the window in the sky.

Ring, ring. "Robert, this
is Robert." "Is this Robert?"
"This is Robert, Robert."

"Yes, Robert," I say, speaking
to my friend Robert One.
"This is Robert Two."

Roberts . . .
Robertness . . .
Three Knights of a Roberthood.

Basketball's the American Game
Because It's Hysterical

"Basketball's the American game because it's hysterical,"
says Lorrie Goldensohn as the players and coaches come
off the bench and the crowd is on its feet yelling and
the Knicks are ahead 97-95 with just over three minutes
to go in the fourth quarter and Perry hits from the side
and Lorrie's husband, Barry, comes downstairs with a
bottle of scotch and a guide to English verse.

"Unless there is
 a new mind, there cannot be a new line," he reads,
refilling our glasses.
"Without invention the line
will never again take on its ancient
divisions . . ."

All evening we have been watching the New York Knicks
battling the Boston Celtics and having a running
argument about free verse, traditional rhyming poetry,
syllabic verse ("What's the point in counting for
counting's sake?"), the critic Hugh Kenner, John
Hollander's *Rhyme's Reason,* the variable foot and
the American idiom.

"In and out by Williams," says the announcer. "He's got
a nose for the basket." The crowd is on its feet
again, roaring.

"We know nothing and can know nothing
but the dance, to dance to a measure
contrapuntally,
satyrically, the tragic foot," Barry continues.

The Celtics race down the court. "Talk about the
green wave coming at you." Bird hits and the Celtics
even the score.

"Basketball's the American game because it's like the
variable foot," says Lorrie. "It's up in the air
all the time. It's quick and the floor is continually
moving and there's this short back-and-forth factor."

"What I like best about the game," I say, "is shutting
my eyes and tuning out the announcer and hearing
Barry read and arguing about poetry and drinking
and listening all the while to the music of
seven-foot black herons in gym shoes, ten giant
gazelles, the stirring squeak of twenty oversize
sneakers on the varnished floor, a floor which
has been carefully and ingeniously miked in advance
for sound."

Hannah

Her third eye is strawberry jam
has a little iris in it
her eyelids
     are red
she's sleepy
     and the milk
     has gone down
     the wrong way.
I've just had breakfast
with the smallest person in the world.

On My Way to the Korean War .

—for President Dwight Eisenhower

On my way to the Korean War,
I never got there.
One summer afternoon in 1952,
I stood instead in the bow
of the attack transport *Menard,*
with an invading force
of 2,000 battle-ready Marines,
watching the sun go down.
Whales and porpoises,
flying fish and things jumping
out of the water.
Phosphoresence—
Honolulu behind us,
Inchon, Korea, and the war ahead.

Crewcut, 18-year-old librarian,
Yeoman 3rd Class, editor
of the ship's newspaper,
I wrote critically if unoriginally
of our commander in chief,
Mr. President,
and how perplexing it was that he
would launch a nuclear-powered submarine
while invoking the Lord,
Crocodile Earthshaker,
Shiva J. Thunderclap,
choosing the occasion to sing
the now famous Song of the Armaments,
the one with the line "weapons for peace":

    O weapons for peace,
    O weapons for peace,
    awh want, awh want
    more weapons for peace!

At sundown, a half-dozen sailors
converged on the bow of the ship
where, composed and silent,
we'd maintain our vigil
until the sun had set.

Careful to avoid being conspicuous,
no flapping or flailing of the arms,
no running, horizontal takeoffs,
one man, then another, stepped out into space,
headed across the water,
moving along as if on threads.
After a while, I did the same:
left my body just as they left theirs.

> In-breathe, out-breathe, and leave,
> in-breathe, out-breathe, and leave.
> Leave your body, leave your body,
> leave your body, leave your body,

we sang as we went out
to where the light went,
and whatever held us to that ship
and its 2,000 battle-ready troops, let go.
So it was, dear friends, I learned to fly.
And so in time must you
and so will the warships,
and the earth itself,
and the sky,
for as the prophet says, the day cometh
when there will be no earth left to leave.

> O me, O my,
> O me, O my,
> goodbye earth, goodbye sky.
> Goodbye, goodbye.

Continuous Topless Strippers

—for Jim Belisle

An eight-speaker sound system,
two continuous topless strippers,
Elvis Presley singing "Early Morning Rain."

Everyone loves television.
And because the management doesn't want
to offend anyone's tastes by omitting

So important an element
in the desired sensory mix—
"The lowest common denominator

"Creates an art form," my friend
mutters into his beer—
the five-foot-by-seven-foot color TV

Is seen on stage backing up the strippers,
the TV little more than a concentration
of bright flashing lights which,

On closer examination, turn out
to be the Six O'clock Evening News.
"Some damned half-deranged diplomat,

"Portfolio this, portfolio that,
is dithering about something or other somewhere
or other for no reason that neither you nor I

"Nor anyone else has any idea." My friend
orders another, and I order another.
The announcer, meanwhile, is selling hangover

Or headache pills and the difficulty we all have
on occasion of falling asleep or eliminating
properly or what happens when we drink too much
     coffee

And that and everything else at last dissolves
the dancers achieving what appears, in fact, to be
a new breakthrough

In negotiations, winning
in the ovation that follows
their performance

Not only our freedom
but the release and freedom
of all hostages.

Sausalito Ferry Poem

"Okay, we're here! Stop scribbling,"
she shouts back at me
climbing down the iron ladder
expecting me to follow.

The boat goes sailing off
to Tiburon,
me with one-half a new poem standing
waving at her from the railing.

"Pink light round your white body,
your blue eyes flashing," I sing
into the wind.
"What's that you're saying? I forgot
to get off?
It's all over now between us?

"All I care about is poetry?
O listen, my love, just listen.
You know that's not true.
I know you'll like this one,
these lines
written exclusively for you."

Four for Love

108,000 Ways of Making Love

Her lips are full, magenta-red
       in color —

Bare-chested, she wears a yellow silk
       loincloth.
I cup my right hand
       under her blue chin
and bend to kiss her,
encircling her waist with my left arm.

Her back to me, she turns

Strings of pearls,
lion-claw necklaces and
rubies and gold round her neck.

Her skin is dark,
       dark as the skin of the blue god.
She has thick, reddish-brown hair
       and brown eyes.

She's wearing garlands
       of fresh wildflowers,
gold rings on every finger,
       red and golden bangles
carved like serpents round
       both ankles.

I stroke her pearly, iridescent thighs,
tenderly smacking
       as she tenderly slaps and smacks me back,

Our bodies etched with scratches
       of our sharp nails

. . . hooting and chirruping
with the brazen nightbirds
gazing in at us
from half-open windows
and doorways

Framed by purple, green,
red-pink twilit bougainvillea.

She presses her big toe
        and also her next-
to-biggest-toe, and the toe
        next to that, and all her other toes,
high up into my crotch
        as I gently guide her with my hand.

I enter her with my mouth
        and she with her mouth
does the same
as I enter her from the front
        and behind,
even as she lowers herself onto my body,
even as I rise to pull her
        to me.
Mirrors installed in the ceilings and walls
        illustrate what we dedicate ourselves to:

Making love in 108,000 ways all at the same time.

Kiss Bite & Moo Softly

— Muse voice is loved woman mumbling.

Going shopping with the muse
you come away buying the right things:
rare books and cashmere pullovers for him,
silk dresses, a gold and amethyst necklace for her.
    Her skin
fair and fine as the yellow
lotus, eyes bright as orbs
of a fawn, well cut with reddish
corners. Bosom hard,
full and high, neck
goodly shaped as the conch
shell. Love seed. Kāma
salila, the water of life.
Swan-like gait. Note
of the Kokila-bird. Kisses
don't interrupt sentences.
    Sleeping
her arms fall into the same
position
    as the Statue of Liberty.

Jealousy

She buys a green corduroy jacket
with a velvet collar
and a label that reads
    Crazy Horse

But tries it on first in the fitting room
where I pull her to me,
reaching up
      under her blouse,
nuzzling her breasts,
stroking her back,
kissing her ears,
sucking on her earlobes,

My hands jealous of my lips,
my lips jealous of my hands

I tell her of my jealousy, and she confesses
to an urge to call me on the phone
at that time of the afternoon
when I'm likely to be at home.

She becomes annoyed
    at my unfaithfulness,
that instead of being there to answer the phone
I lie beside her,
    stroking
    exploring
our lips joined,
until at last
rolling together on the fitting room floor—

"I want to speak with you," she breathes,
"and have you all to myself.
I want to hear you call for me and moan.

Lover, oh lover," she sighs at last,
"I want to call now and tell my lover,
oh, my lover, oh, my lover."

For Gloria on Her 60th Birthday, or Looking for Love in Merriam-Webster

"Beautiful, splendid, magnificent,
delightful, charming, appealing,"
          says the dictionary.
And that's how I start . . . But I hear her say,
"Make it less glorious and more Gloria."

Imperious, composed, skeptical, serene,
lustrous, irreverent,
she's marked by glory, she attracts glory
"Glory," I say, "Glory, Glory."

"Is there a hallelujah in there?"
she asks, when I read her lines one and two.
"Not yet," I say, looking up from my books.
She protests, "Writing a poem isn't the same

"As *really* attending to me." "But it's for
your birthday," I say. Pouting,
playfully cross, "That's the price you pay
when your love's a poet."

She has chestnut-colored hair,
old-fashioned Clara Bow lips,
moist brown eyes . . .
          arms outstretched, head thrown back
she glides toward me and into her seventh decade.

Her name means "to adore,"
"to rejoice, to be jubilant,
to magnify and honor as in worship, to give or ascribe glory—"
          my love, O Gloria, I do, I do.

34 Poets Named Robert

1. ROBERT FROST, ROBERT LOWELL, ROBERT SERVICE . . .

Yes, I met Robert Frost and Robert Lowell and Robert Creeley,
and Robert Duncan and Robert Mezey, Robert Bly and Robert
Peterson, appeared in *A Controversy of Poets: An Anthology of
Contemporary American Poetry* edited by Robert Kelly, but not
in *New Poets of England and America* edited by Robert Pack, ad-
mire the work of Robert Bridges, Robert Browning, Robert
Burns, Robert Dana, Robert Finch, Robert Graves, Robert
Hass, Robert Herrick, Robert Hogg, Robert Huff, Robert Lax,
Robert McDowell, Robert McGovern, Robert Peters, Robert
Pinsky, Robert Southey, and Robert Louis Stevenson, and even
performed in taverns and coffee houses in London, Ontario, and
in Toronto at Major Robert's Restaurant—near the intersection
of Major and Robert streets—with Canadian poets Robert
Priest and Robert Zend, the three of us, billed as The Three
Roberts, dedicating our readings to CBC Radio's Robert Weaver
and Robert Prowse, to the literary critic Robert Fulford, with
half a dedication to my friend John Robert Colombo, and to
Robert Service.

2. "I'M NOT GOING TO GO ON LIKE THIS . . ."

But as each of my four wives explained, patiently or otherwise,
over a period of three decades, "Robert, it doesn't pay. Robert,
there's no future in it. I'm not going to go on like this . . ." and
"Robert, doesn't it depress you to go into libraries and see all
those poetry books by all those other writers named Robert,
even the ones not named Robert, that practically no one on
earth is going to read?" "Well, yes, it's true it doesn't pay. And
it's true there's no future in it. And it does depress me that prac-
tically no one in America wants to read poetry, and that's why I
taught for fourteen years and even took a job writing software
user manuals. But then, unable to let go of what I'd done for 35
years, resigned in order to go back and write some more poetry.

"And today I think of you as I re-read this morning's mail.

"Three letters. One from Robert Priest, the Canadian poet. He writes of the death by drowning of the poet Robert Billings, and the deaths also of poets b.p. nichol, Gwendolyn MacEwen, and Milton Acorn. And Earle Birney, he says, who, at 75 was seen by the editor of *New: American & Canadian Poetry* in a Toronto rainstorm in the throes of love running up Yonge Street bearing flowers for his 35-year-old sweetheart; Birney who, at 79 fell out of a tree from which he'd been trying to dislodge a kite, and who, not long after, recovering from an injured hip, resumed cycling on a regular basis at breakneck speed through a North Toronto cemetery; Birney, he says, alive and in his eighties, has visitors who read him his poems, poems that, when Birney hears them, with impaired memory, he enjoys, though he is unable to understand he is the author of those poems.

"Letter #2: Nicky Drumbolis, proprietor of a Toronto bookstore, writes that his rent has gone up $700 a month, that he must give up the store, and that he is "earnestly clearing stock for the big move."

"And the publisher of my last book writes that he has become part-owner of Omega Apparel, a business to which he now devotes all his time. He's not publishing any more poetry by anyone these days, only neckties."

3. "ROBERT, THIS IS ROBERT. IS THIS ROBERT?"

I drift off at my computer and dream of Robert Zend, whose heart gave out four years ago, and of Robert Priest and Earle Birney, and in the dream I see myself reading my favorite Birney poems to Birney,

> I met a lady
>   on a lazy street
> hazel eyes
>   and little plush feet

her legs swam by
   like lovely trout
eyes were trees
   where boys leant out

(from *The Hazel Bough*)

and he is lucid as my father before his heart stopped at 82, and just before I wake, Birney tells me I am a cross between Halley's comet and Rip Van Winkle the way I go off to England, France, Mexico, Canada, and then, years later, return, meeting the sons and daughters of the people, of the Roberts, for example, I once knew, and that that is what poems are supposed to do, and that I have been living more like a poem in a sense than a man with his feet on the ground, and that in the time that remains I should be living more like a man with his feet on the ground and less like a poem.

4. FLASHBACK — THE MAN IN THE CELLOPHANE PAJAMA BOTTOMS

6 AM. I'm getting dressed to drive over Highway 17 to Palo Alto. Half asleep, naked, I am pulling on my trousers. It's still dark and, switching on the light, I see they are not trousers at all, but cellophane pajama bottoms . . . regenerated cellulose, like what smokers tear off packages of cigarettes. Late for work, walking down the front steps of our house, heading for the car with a tea kettle to boil water, I think better of it.

"Today I'm going to stay in Santa Cruz and boil water at home."

Handing me a cup of tea, reaching for the massage oil, helping me off with my thin, transparent pajamas, my love murmurs softly, "You can boil water and write pot boilers right here."

5. HOW TO BE A MILLIONAIRE

"How come the millionaire owner of a newspaper got by paying me—and two other editors—$1,700 a month to write, edit, take

125

photographs, create captions, lay out and produce three separate editions of the rag by ourselves, working up to 19 hours a day?"

"Because really successful entrepreneurs know how to screw people and make them like it," says my love. "That's how you make money in America."

Smart woman. And next she informs me she's fed up with my lavish, celebratory love poems:

> . . . Her skin
> fair and fine as the yellow
> lotus, eyes bright as orbs
> of a fawn,
>   . . . Bosom hard,
> full and high . . .

She wants tougher poems, she says, poems about the wrinkles on her face, the imperfections of her character, her crossness, her bluntness, her imperiousness, impatience, her struggle to lose rather than to gain weight. I'm puzzled. How can I write about her wrinkles if I can't find any? Or her crossness when she is so seldom cross? Or her weight, when it doesn't bother me at all? Then, softening, remarking how my poverty makes her feel young ("It's as if we're in our twenties and just starting out"), she inspires me to make money.

"I'll make lots of money," I promise, "and I'll do it without screwing people. And to prove it, I'll start now, just as soon as I finish this poem."

Acknowledgments

Grateful acknowledgment is made to the editors of the following publications for permission to reprint many of the poems in this book: *Airon 9* (Buenos Aires), *Ambit* (London), *Antioch Review, Approach Magazine, Arts In Society* (Madison, Wisconsin), *The Activist* (Oberlin College), *Artes / Letres Dialogs* (Mexico City), *Beloit Poetry Journal, Best Articles & Stories, Carleton Miscellany, Center* (New York), *Chelsea* (New York), *Chicago Review, Contemporary Verse II* (University of Manitoba), *Cross Canada Writers Quarterly* (Toronto), *Denver Quarterly, Descant, El Corno Emplumado* (Mexico City), *Epoch* (Cornell University), *The Etruscan* (New South Wales, Australia), *Exposicion Exhaustiva De La Nueva Poesia Galeria* (Montevideo), *Equal Time* (New York), *Extensions* (New York), *The Fiddlehead* (New Brunswick), *From A Window* (Tucson), *Galley Sail Review, Greenfield Review* (Greenfield Center, New York), *Hawaii Review* (Honolulu), *Hudson Review, The Humanist, Inkstone* (Bowling Green, Ohio), *The Iowa Review, Karaki* (Victoria, B.C.), *Kayak* (Santa Cruz), *Malahat Review* (Victoria, B.C.), *The Martlet* (Victoria, B.C.), *Massachusetts Review, Matrix* (London), *Michigan Quarterly Review, Mt. Shasta Selections* (MSS), *The Nation, New Mexico Quarterly, New Orleans Poetry Journal, New Work #1, The New Yorker, The New York Times, The North American Review, Northern Light* (University of Manitoba), *The Northstone Review* (Minneapolis), *The Paris Review, Pearl* (Denmark), *Penny Poems, Perspective* (St. Louis), *Poetry Chicago, Poetry Toronto, Poetry Australia, Poetry Northwest, Prism International* (Vancouver, B.C.), *Quarterly Review of Literature, Rampike* (York University), *The Santa Cruz Sentinel, Shenandoah, Stone* (Ithaca, New York), *Signal Hill Broadsides* (Victoria, B.C.), *Tambourine* (St. Louis),

Transatlantic Review (London), *Triquarterly* (Evanston, Illinois), *Tuatara* (Victoria, B.C.), *UCSC Student Guide* (Santa Cruz), *Waves* (Toronto), *West Coast Works* (Vancouver, B.C.), *Wild Dog, Zahir* (Portsmouth, New Hampshire).

Some of these poems have been recorded by Western Michigan University's Aural Press (1005), the Library of Congress, and National Public Radio (New Letters on the Air, University of Missouri).

Others have appeared in the following anthologies: *A Controversy of Poets: An Anthology of Contemporary American Poets; The Chicago Review Anthology; The Contemporary American Poets: American Poetry Since 1940; Heartland: Poets of the Midwest; Illinois Poetry; Inside Outer Space: New Poems of the Space Age; Inventions for Imaginative Thinking; Lighthouse Point: An Anthology of Santa Cruz Writers; Midland: 25 Years of Fiction and Poetry; New Yorker Book of Poems; The Now Voices; Oxford Book of Light Verse; Penguin Book of Animal Poetry; Riverside Poetry III; Silver Screen: Neue Amerikanische Lyrik; Some Haystacks Don't Even Have Any Needle; Sports Poems; The Practical Imagination; The Space Atlas; Tesseracts: Canadian Science Fiction; The Treasure of Our Tongue; The Voice That Is Great Within Us; To Say the Least: Canadian Poets from A to Z;* and *Where Is Vietnam?: American Poets Respond.*

R.D. Brinkmann and Peter Behrens translated some of these poems into German in a volume titled *Silver Screen: Neue Amerikanische Lyrik*, Kiepenheuer & Witsch, Köln. Others were translated into Spanish by Madela Ezcurra and Eduardo Costa and appeared in *Airon 9*, Buenos Aires.